COUPLE'S GOALS JOURNAL

Couple's
GOALS
JOURNAL

52 Weeks
of Prompts and Activities
to Track and Celebrate
Your Relationship Goals

Tara Blair Ball

**ROCKRIDGE
PRESS**

First Rockridge Press trade paperback edition 2022

Rockridge Press and the Rockridge Press logo are trademarks or registered trademarks of Callisto Media Inc. and/or its affiliates in the United States and other countries and may not be used without written permission.

For general information on our other products and services, please contact our Customer Care Department within the United States at (866) 744-2665, or outside the United States at (510) 253-0500.

Paperback ISBN: 978-1-63878-254-4

Manufactured in the United States of America

Interior and Cover Designer: Scott Petrower
Art Producer: Hannah Dickerson
Editor: Katherine De Chant
Production Editor: Dylan Julian
Production Manager: Lanore Coloprisco

All images used under license from iStock.com, Shutterstock.com and The Noun Project, except for the following: © Sarah Rebar, p. 149.

10 9 8 7 6 5 4 3 2 1 0

Throughout this journal, you will notice there are blank spaces for either Partner 1 or Partner 2. Start by selecting who will be Partner 1 and who will be Partner 2. After you have chosen, each person should sign their name next to their number.

....

....

Introduction

As a certified relationship coach, I've advised hundreds of clients on how to have happier and healthier relationships. One practice that I've always recommended is working together to develop relationship goals. When we want to be promoted, get fit, retire early, or attain something else, we are usually able to achieve those dreams by first setting goals. We are much more likely to achieve something if we make it our intention and take actionable steps to reach it.

The same is true for couples. When you and your partner set goals, you're planning a future together. The simple act of sitting down and working through this process will help you make progress toward your desired future.

This journal will help you and your partner set and work toward *relationship* goals. Relationship goals are ones you and your partner create to improve your relationship. Healthy relationships have a strong foundation of love, trust, and respect, so it can be helpful to set goals related to one of these three aspects.

As your relationship evolves, it can be easy to become complacent or lose focus on your foundation of love. You and your partner may forget to express gratitude to each other or to be intentional about having date nights. In fact, setting regular date nights is a goal that helps improve the love in the relationship.

Cultivating trust in your relationship goes hand in hand with honesty and communication. Our partner's trust in us can be broken if we withhold, fudge, minimize, or outright lie. We can also struggle to trust because of past betrayals, whether they were in our current relationship or not. As you work toward being trustworthy and trusting in your relationship, your goal could be to learn how to communicate more openly and honestly with your partner. It can be scary to share that you're feeling insecure, uncomfortable, or afraid, but we build safety in relationships by doing just that.

Respect in a relationship involves recognizing that you and your partner are equals. Working toward having respect in a relationship can look like learning how to fight fairly (every couple will argue, but we should treat our partner with respect even when we're mad at them). Respect in a relationship can also look like honoring each other's boundaries; supporting each other's goals, dreams, interests, and hobbies; compromising; and taking time to really listen to and value what the other says. Any of these would be healthy goals to improve the respect in your relationship.

Having shared relationship goals can help solidify that you and your partner are a team, ensure that you're on the same page, and make you much more likely to achieve those goals. Working toward your goals together will help you develop a healthier and happier relationship.

How to Use This Journal

In most relationships, there are planners and "pants-ers." Planners are just like they sound. They write to-do lists and complete them diligently. Pants-ers, on the other hand, prefer to fly by the seat of their pants. They'll choose spontaneity over list writing any day.

This journal is for *both* types of people. This journal is a 52-week goal tracker for couples, with clear exercises for goal setting, goal tracking, and planning creative date nights.

Each prompt will be followed by two sets of lines so you and your partner can each write your answers separately. This way you can both write honestly, track your progress, and have a wonderful keepsake once the year is completed. If you're not much of a writer, don't feel like you have to write out complete sentences. Bullet points will do! Also, not every prompt will require you to write. Some will ask you to draw or check off boxes. One of you can also agree to be the "scribe" for the two of you.

Part 1 of this journal will introduce you to the SMART framework for setting goals. If we don't have specific, measurable, attainable, relevant, and timed goals, we're much less likely to be successful in meeting those goals. Applying the SMART goal method can help you and your partner refine your goals and assess how you will reach them in a way that's unique to the both of you.

After you learn about what makes a great goal, you will brainstorm. This will be your opportunity to write out your goals, refine them, and dig into what you want to achieve in your relationship in the coming year.

Part 2 is the tracking section. Once you and your partner have your overall goals, you will take time every week to decide what you want to work on. When we break our goals into manageable chunks (like a week at a time), they're much less likely to feel overwhelming. There will also be cute prompts that will help remind you why your relationship is great.

Set aside a weekly block of time to go through this journal. Make it something you'll both look forward to by adding special touches like snacks or candles. Use these dates to celebrate your hard work and add an extra dose of fun to the goal-setting process. Sporadically throughout this journal you'll encounter Save the Date (Night) cards inviting you to plan a cute date night. You can use these cards as prompts to plan your next date then and there or as inspiration on mixing things up for your weekly date nights.

Every four weeks, there will be a check-in. During your check-ins, you'll have the chance to reflect back over the previous four weeks and evaluate how things have gone. You'll consider what did or didn't work, what needs to be adjusted or changed, what you enjoyed, and what you struggled with.

Now you're ready to begin. Have fun!

Part I
SMART-er Together

The SMART system is a clear and effective way to help you and your partner achieve your goals. This system was developed by George Doran, Arthur Miller, and James Cunningham, and uses an acronym that helps ensure your goals are succinct and manageable. SMART stands for:

Specific: direct and simple

Measurable: quantifiable and able to be measured

Attainable: realistic and within reach

Relevant: reasonable and pertinent

Time-bound: deadline-specific

Being able to refine your goals based on this acronym makes it possible for you to hone your efforts, manage your time and resources, and increase the likelihood that you will achieve your desired outcomes.

Part 1 will help you and your partner create relationship goals that are specific, measurable, attainable, relevant, and time-bound. The following prompts will guide you in using this system effectively to get what you want out of your relationship.

SAVE THE DATE (Night)

For this first date, order takeout from your favorite restaurant and camp out on the couch. Use this date to complete part 1 of the journal and use future dates to complete the weekly prompts in part 2.

SPECIFIC

Specific goals are clear and direct. This allows you to focus your efforts and home in on what's important. To make a goal specific, think about answering the following questions:

What do you want to achieve?

Why do you want to achieve it?

Who needs to be involved?

Which resources will be required to achieve it?

For example, if you'd like to improve communication in your relationship, what specifically could you work on? Are there books or resources available to help you learn how to communicate more effectively?

How will you make sure your goals are specific?

1

2

MEASURABLE

Measurable goals have benchmarks, deadlines, or time specifications to help you know you've accomplished them. You know that a goal is measurable if you can clearly track your progress. Making sure your goals are measurable will help you stay inspired and motivated and allow you to assess whether you're still on the right track.

For example, if your goal is "I want to communicate more often with my partner," you could make it measurable by saying, "I will call my partner two times a week when I'm out of town."

How can you make your goals measurable? What types of criteria might you use to measure them?

1

2

ATTAINABLE

To ensure you're not stretching yourself too thin or putting unrealistic expectations on yourself, each of your goals should be attainable. Think carefully about your goals and ask yourself the following questions:

How will I be able to accomplish this goal?

Are there any responsibilities, time constraints, or budget concerns that may make achieving this goal difficult?

For example, if you'd like to have more regular date nights with your partner, it may be too difficult to have a date night *every* week. Instead, it might make more sense to have a date twice a month.

How can you make your goals attainable and realistic, considering your other commitments?

1
_____
_____
_____
_____
_____

2
_____
_____
_____
_____
_____

RELEVANT

Relevant goals are ones that clearly matter to you and make sense for you individually. For example, let's say you and your partner would like to save money to make a large purchase together. It will be more impactful if each partner sets their own goal toward achieving this end, a goal that homes in on each person's individual desires related to the goal.

To assess if a goal is relevant, ask yourself:

Is this goal meaningful to me? Why?

Does it make sense for me to pursue it now?

Relevant goals will help you and your partner create a plan for a shared end while still allowing each of you to be responsible for your own part.

How can you make sure your goals are relevant and personal to you?

1

2

TIMED

Timed goals need to have specific time frames that dictate when you'll complete your goal. This will also help you measure your success along the way and stay accountable. Deadlines can help you track your progress and make it more likely that you will achieve your goals.

To make sure your goals are timed, choose a start and end date for each one. The time frames you select should be not only reasonable (considering your other constraints) but also motivating (not so crunched that you feel stressed that you won't be able to get it done in time).

Write down some ideas for ensuring that your goals will have specific time frames or deadlines?

1

2

PARTNER #1 GOALS

Now that we've addressed every aspect of the SMART system, write out
your relationship goals.

1

PARTNER #2 GOALS

Now that we've addressed every aspect of the SMART system, write out your relationship goals.

2

Part II
Goal for It!

Each week, you and your partner will decide on weekly goals. You can decide to each work on a shared goal, or work on individual goals. You will take time each week to consider your goal and what you'll need to be successful working toward it. The tracking pages that follow will help you do just that.

Remember, each of your goals should be attainable, so it can be helpful to break your larger goals into smaller chunks. Further, the more specific you can be, the better! This journal is also meant to help you appreciate your relationship and your partner, so there will be creative prompts that inspire you to consider their special qualities and the joy you share together.

Every four weeks, you will have a check-in in addition to your usual prompts. This check-in will help you look at your progress overall and celebrate how far you've come. This is also an opportunity to decide if something isn't working and make changes accordingly.

WEEK 1

Date ....

To work toward my goal, this week I will . . .

1 ....
....
....
....

2 ....
....
....

To help me be successful, I will need the following for myself and/or from my partner . . .

1 ....
....
....
....

2 ....
....
....

If your partner were a car, what kind would they be? Are they a flashy sports car or more of a classic pickup truck? Would they have leather seats or a great sound system? Share your answer with your partner and see if they agree.

1 ....

....

....

2 ....

....

....

Imagine that you and your partner are a superhero duo. What powers do you have, and what is your origin story about how you got them? Do you use your powers for good, or are you super*villains*?

1 ....

....

....

2 ....

....

....

WEEK 2   Date ....

To work toward my goal, this week I will . . .

1 ....

....

....

....

2 ....

....

....

....

To help me be successful, I will need the following for myself and/or from my partner . . .

1 ....

....

....

....

2 ....

....

....

....

I love having my partner in my life because . . .

1

2

Imagine you're going on a trip with your partner. Would you rather sunbathe on the beach, go on a hike, or peruse an art gallery? Circle the icon that best represents the kind of trip you'd love to take with your partner. If one doesn't match, draw one that does! Then jot down a few destinations you'd like to visit with them.

1

2

WEEK 3

Date ....

To work toward my goal, this week I will . . .

1 ....

....

....

....

2 ....

....

....

....

To help me be successful, I will need the following for myself and/or from my partner . . .

1 ....

....

....

....

2 ....

....

....

....

Which of the seven adjectives below best describes how you feel about your partner on a regular basis? (Check all that apply.)

1

☐ **happy**

☐ **horny**

☐ **tickled**

☐ **inspired**

☐ **supported**

☐ **warm**

☐ **romantic**

2

☐ **happy**

☐ **horny**

☐ **tickled**

☐ **inspired**

☐ **supported**

☐ **warm**

☐ **romantic**

SAVE THE DATE (Night)

Re-create your first date! Where did you go together, and what outfits did you wear? Try to re-create as many elements as possible. Ask each other questions like "If you had one day to live, what would you do?"

What job do you think your partner would be great at (that they don't currently do), and why? Maybe their attention to detail would make them a great teacher or investment banker. Draw a picture of your partner doing that job. Not an artist? Make it silly! Stick figures are encouraged.

1

WEEK 4

Date ....

To work toward my goal, this week I will . . .

....

....

....

....

....

....

To help me be successful, I will need the following for myself and/or from my partner . . .

....

....

....

2

....

....

....

Brainstorm a short list of things you'd love to do for your partner. Then brainstorm a few things you'd love for them to do for you on a regular basis. These might be sending a good-morning or good-night text, hugging or kissing each other goodbye, cooking a meal together, or giving little treats.

1 ....

....

....

....

2 ....

....

....

....

Fill in the blanks (with silly or serious answers) for the following sentence.

1 "When I first saw you, you looked

....(adjective).

You smelled like a ....(noun),

and I was most drawn to your ....(noun).

2 "When I first saw you, you looked

....(adjective).

You smelled like a ....(noun),

and I was most drawn to your ....(noun)."

CHECK-IN

Think about your progress over the last four weeks. On the line below, list several adjectives that describe your feelings. Then rate the last four weeks on a scale of one to five (five being great).

1 2 3 4 5

1. Over the last four weeks, what have you most enjoyed about working toward your goals? What can you celebrate or feel good about?

2. What has been the most difficult for you? Is there anything you tried that didn't work? Did anything disappoint or surprise you?

3. How do you feel about your partner today? Is there anything you'd like to do differently in your relationship or in reaching your goals over the next four weeks?

CHECK-IN

Think about your progress over the last four weeks. On the line below, list several adjectives that describe your feelings. Then rate the last four weeks on a scale of one to five (five being great).

1 2 3 4 5

....

1. Over the last four weeks, what have you most enjoyed about working toward your goals? What can you celebrate or feel good about?

....

....

....

2. What has been the most difficult for you? Is there anything you tried that didn't work? Did anything disappoint or surprise you?

....

....

....

3. How do you feel about your partner today? Is there anything you'd like to do differently in your relationship or in reaching your goals over the next four weeks?

....

....

....

WEEK 5

Date ....

To work toward my goal, this week I will . . .

....
....
....
....

....
....
....

To help me be successful, I will need the following for myself and/or from my partner . . .

....
....
....
....

....
....
....

What are some songs that make you think of your partner? Brainstorm a list, then create a playlist and give it to your partner! Play both of your playlists the next time you take a long road trip or during your next at-home date night.

1

2

If money didn't matter, what would you love for you and your partner to do? Jot down a few ideas and get their feedback.

1

2

Date

To work toward my goal, this week I will . . .

1

2

To help me be successful, I will need the following for myself and/or from my partner . . .

1

2

Unscramble the following words. Each answer refers to a sign of a good relationship.

nmcciuoniatom ....

sienskdn ....

cetsper ....

sytnheo ....

ttrsu ....

edncpenniede ....

ovel ....

sesfuyallnp ....

tgenaremouenc ....

protups ....

mepayth ....

raec ....

rntoiapecpai ....

snovreeifsg ....

edtiaurtg ....

Draw your partner, making it as accurate as possible. If that's too much pressure, you can doodle a silly portrait or things that make you think of them. If drawing isn't your thing, write down some adjectives that you'd use to describe your partner to a stranger. Maybe smart, hilarious, sexy . . .

1

2

WEEK 7

Date ....

To work toward my goal, this week I will . . .

1 ....

....

....

....

2 ....

....

....

....

To help me be successful, I will need the following for myself and/or from my partner . . .

1 ....

....

....

....

2 ....

....

....

....

Grab a sheet of paper and write out twenty-five little acts of love. These could be back rubs, small gift ideas, or snacks you like to eat. Clip them out, fold them, and put them in a jar. This is your "love jar." Whenever your partner wants to show they love you, they can pick something from your jar!

Which movie star would you say that your partner most resembles, and why?

1

2

SAVE THE DATE (Night)

Set a budget (think $25 a piece), then go to a large store in your area. Your mission is to split up and each buy five gifts for your partner. Come back together and laugh at what you got each other.

Date

To work toward my goal, this week I will . . .

1

2

To help me be successful, I will need the following for myself and/or from my partner . . .

1

2

What are some traditions you'd like to start with your partner? Maybe Taco Tuesdays or a weekly hike?

①

②

For each category below, write out three desirable options. Then let your partner give you a fourth terrible option for each category. Randomly pick a number between three and ten. Count out that many of your options and strike out what you land on. Continue until all but one option in each category is crossed out, then circle the final answers and read them out. That's your fortune! Repeat the process so both partners get a turn.

CITIES	JOBS	SALARIES

CARS	PETS	# OF KIDS

2

CITIES	JOBS	SALARIES

CARS	PETS	# OF KIDS

CHECK-IN

Think about your progress over the last four weeks. On the line below, list several adjectives that describe your feelings. Then rate the last four weeks on a scale of one to five (five being great).

1 2 3 4 5

....

1. Over the last four weeks, what have you most enjoyed about working toward your goals? What can you celebrate or feel good about?

....

....

....

2. What has been the most difficult for you? Is there anything you tried that didn't work? Did anything disappoint or surprise you?

....

....

....

3. How do you feel about your partner today? Is there anything you'd like to do differently in your relationship or in reaching your goals over the next four weeks?

....

....

....

CHECK-IN

Think about your progress over the last four weeks. On the line below, list several adjectives that describe your feelings. Then rate the last four weeks on a scale of one to five (five being great).

1 2 3 4 5

....

1. Over the last four weeks, what have you most enjoyed about working toward your goals? What can you celebrate or feel good about?

....

....

....

2. What has been the most difficult for you? Is there anything you tried that didn't work? Did anything disappoint or surprise you?

....

....

....

3. How do you feel about your partner today? Is there anything you'd like to do differently in your relationship or in reaching your goals over the next four weeks?

....

....

....

Date

To work toward my goal, this week I will . . .

1

2

To help me be successful, I will need the following for myself and/or from my partner . . .

1

2

According to psychologist Susan Orenstein, a relationship mission statement is "a declaration created and agreed upon by the couple that guides their principles, goals, and values." What would be yours? Here's an example: "We agree to build a relationship where we love, care, and respect each other."

1. ....

2. ....

Make a list of your partner's favorite things: candy, chips, gum, dessert, ice cream, alcohol, and snacks. Then circle three to four that you can surprise them with soon!

1. ....

2. ....

Date

To work toward my goal, this week I will . . .

1

2

To help me be successful, I will need the following for myself and/or from my partner . . .

1

2

Start a couple's bucket list! Circle two or three activities that you'd love to try with your partner.

- **Get a couples massage**

- **Go stargazing**

- **Play Twister**

- **Learn how to dance**

- **Go bungee-jumping or cliff-diving**

- **Volunteer together**

- **Ride a Ferris wheel together**

- **Take a workout class together**

Who was your partner's role model growing up? Who do they most look up to today? If you don't know, ask them!

SAVE THE DATE (Night)

Learn how to cook a recipe together. Register for a cooking class in your area or pick a recipe and do it together. You can even find a YouTube video or online cooking course to try out.

Date ....

To work toward my goal, this week I will . . .

1 ....
....
....
....

2 ....
....
....
....

To help me be successful, I will need the following for myself and/or from my partner . . .

1 ....
....
....
....

2 ....
....
....
....

Write out two truths and one lie, then see if your partner can guess your lie. Be as convincing as possible and try to see if you can trip your partner up!

1

2

If your home went up in flames, what would you want to grab as you were running out? What do you think your partner would prioritize? Compare your answers.

1

2

Date ....

To work toward my goal, this week I will . . .

1

2

To help me be successful, I will need the following for myself and/or from my partner . . .

1

2

What have you always wanted to do with your partner, but haven't gotten around to yet? Maybe you'd like to sample a new restaurant, explore a new place, or try something new in the bedroom. If your partner doesn't know, this is a great opportunity to tell them.

1 ....

....

....

....

2 ....

....

....

....

Would you rather . . .

Win the lottery or live twenty years longer?

1 .... **2** ....

Learn a new language or a new instrument?

1 .... **2** ....

Have an extra hour of sleep or alone time?

1 .... **2** ....

Have new clothes or a new car?

1 .... **2** ....

CHECK-IN

Think about your progress over the last four weeks. On the line below, list several adjectives that describe your feelings. Then rate the last four weeks on a scale of one to five (five being great).

1 2 3 4 5

1. Over the last four weeks, what have you most enjoyed about working toward your goals? What can you celebrate or feel good about?

2. What has been the most difficult for you? Is there anything you tried that didn't work? Did anything disappoint or surprise you?

3. How do you feel about your partner today? Is there anything you'd like to do differently in your relationship or in reaching your goals over the next four weeks?

Think about your progress over the last four weeks. On the line below, list several adjectives that describe your feelings. Then rate the last four weeks on a scale of one to five (five being great).

1 2 3 4 5

....

1. Over the last four weeks, what have you most enjoyed about working toward your goals? What can you celebrate or feel good about?

....

....

....

2. What has been the most difficult for you? Is there anything you tried that didn't work? Did anything disappoint or surprise you?

....

....

....

3. How do you feel about your partner today? Is there anything you'd like to do differently in your relationship or in reaching your goals over the next four weeks?

....

....

....

Date ....

To work toward my goal, this week I will . . .

1

2

To help me be successful, I will need the following for myself and/or from my partner . . .

1

2

What is your partner's contact name in your phone? Retitle it to something cute like "The Best Hubby" or "Girlfriend of the Year." Add a few emojis that represent their new title.

1 ....

....

....

2 ....

....

....

If your partner were arrested for something silly, what would it be for? Jaywalking? Forgetting to update their car registration? If you can't think of anything, make it up—like "takes too long to get ready" or "always loses their wallet."

1 ....

....

....

....

2 ....

....

....

To work toward my goal, this week I will . . .

....

....

....

....

....

....

....

To help me be successful, I will need the following for myself and/or from my partner . . .

....

....

....

....

....

....

....

See if you can answer the following questions about your partner without asking them. After you're done, compare answers.

My partner's best friends are . . .

1 .... **2** ....

My partner's dream is to . . .

1 .... **2** ....

My partner's least favorite relatives are . . .

1 .... **2** ....

My partner is currently stressed about . . .

1 .... **2** ....

My partner thinks my best quality is . . .

1 .... **2** ....

If you could have any musician or band put on a show for your birthday party, who would it be? Who do you think your partner would choose?

1 ....

....

2 ....

....

Date

To work toward my goal, this week I will . . .

1

2

To help me be successful, I will need the following for myself and/or from my partner . . .

1

2

Imagine you could go back in time to before you ever met your partner. What advice would you give yourself?

1

2

Think back to the details of your very first date with your partner—what you ate, what you wore, where you went, or what you did. Doodle a few things you remember in the space below. You could also draw how your face looked the first time you saw them.

2

To work toward my goal, this week I will . . .

To help me be successful, I will need the following for myself and/or from my partner . . .

Create your own scavenger hunt! Write a list of ten items that you know are nearby. Then exchange your list with your partner and see who can find all the items on their partner's list first.

1

2

Would your partner rather . . .

Go to the beach or the mountains?

1 .... **2** ....

Eat chocolate or vanilla ice cream?

1 .... **2** ....

Stay home or dine out?

1 .... **2** ....

Watch TV or read books?

1 .... **2** ....

Eat pizza or burgers?

1 .... **2** ....

Drink wine or beer?

1 .... **2** ....

Have a cat or a dog?

1 .... **2** ....

SAVE THE DATE (Night)

Pick a board or video game (either one of your favorites or a brand-new one), get yourself some tasty beverages and snacks, then start playing! Make up fun "prizes" for whoever wins each round.

1 CHECK-IN

Think about your progress over the last four weeks. On the line below, list several adjectives that describe your feelings. Then rate the last four weeks on a scale of one to five (five being great).

1 2 3 4 5

1. Over the last four weeks, what have you most enjoyed about working toward your goals? What can you celebrate or feel good about?

2. What has been the most difficult for you? Is there anything you tried that didn't work? Did anything disappoint or surprise you?

3. How do you feel about your partner today? Is there anything you'd like to do differently in your relationship or in reaching your goals over the next four weeks?

CHECK-IN

Think about your progress over the last four weeks. On the line below, list several adjectives that describe your feelings. Then rate the last four weeks on a scale of one to five (five being great).

1 2 3 4 5

....

1. Over the last four weeks, what have you most enjoyed about working toward your goals? What can you celebrate or feel good about?

....

....

....

2. What has been the most difficult for you? Is there anything you tried that didn't work? Did anything disappoint or surprise you?

....

....

....

3. How do you feel about your partner today? Is there anything you'd like to do differently in your relationship or in reaching your goals over the next four weeks?

....

....

....

Date

To work toward my goal, this week I will . . .

1

2

To help me be successful, I will need the following for myself and/or from my partner . . .

1

2

Play truth or dare with your partner! In the space below, brainstorm potential truth questions and dare challenges. Then let them pick one truth and one dare to do.

1

2

What's something your partner does that you think is great but that you haven't told them about recently? Maybe they always take out the trash, or you really appreciate their glass-half-full attitude.

1

2

WEEK 18

To work toward my goal, this week I will . . .

1

2

To help me be successful, I will need the following for myself and/or from my partner . . .

1

2

What are the things you love most about your partner's physical appearance? Maybe it's their height, the way they style their hair, or their piercing eyes. Write an ode to your favorite feature. Extra points for rhyming lines, like "Your butt is so sexy that it just wrecks me."

1

2

Imagine your partner as a superhero and draw their costume in the space below. Don't forget to include if they'd wear a mask or a cape!

1

2

WEEK 19

To work toward my goal, this week I will . . .

1 ....

....

....

....

2 ....

....

....

....

To help me be successful, I will need the following for myself and/or from my partner . . .

1 ....

....

....

....

2 ....

....

....

....

Are you an over- or underbuyer? An overbuyer tends to have multiple packs of toilet paper while an underbuyer will use up every last bit of toothpaste before buying a new one. Which is your partner?

Circle the emoji that best fits you, then write your name under the emoji. Next, choose one for your partner. Compare your choices! If your favorite emojis aren't included, draw them in the space provided.

Date ....

To work toward my goal, this week I will . . .

1

2

To help me be successful, I will need the following for myself and/or from my partner . . .

1

2

Do you have a favorite iconic TV comedy, like *Friends* or *The Office*? Choose one, decide which character you are most like, and describe why. Which character is your partner most like? Describe a scene where both characters interact, and how that reminds you of your relationship.

1

2

There are twelve relationship character traits located in the word search below. Can you work together to find them all?

vulnerability **attractive** **romantic**
openness **intimacy** **chemistry**
loyal **personable** **maturity**
interesting **funny** **warm**

P	E	R	S	O	N	A	B	L	E	M	Q	I	R	J
Y	V	E	N	C	D	Y	H	O	H	C	O	N	O	O
X	R	U	W	M	K	K	G	C	P	H	H	T	M	K
D	A	G	L	M	C	D	S	J	L	E	T	I	A	O
I	S	R	M	N	F	T	L	W	O	M	M	M	N	M
O	N	I	T	A	E	B	V	Z	Y	I	W	A	T	A
P	W	T	Q	S	T	R	O	G	A	S	A	C	I	T
E	V	A	E	A	B	U	A	Y	L	T	R	Y	C	T
N	Y	L	Y	R	X	L	R	B	E	R	M	B	I	R
N	D	Z	U	I	E	G	I	I	I	Y	I	A	Z	A
E	J	L	F	A	D	S	J	K	T	L	S	P	C	C
S	P	X	M	V	K	G	T	J	D	Y	I	F	S	T
S	C	J	T	J	V	S	A	I	D	D	D	T	E	I
Z	K	B	F	U	N	N	Y	L	N	H	F	X	Y	V
T	F	X	S	Q	U	C	C	Y	W	G	L	P	C	E

SAVE THE DATE (Night)

Role-play can be super fun and flirty, and you can do it at home or out. Pick a character you'd like to dress up as or act like, and have a meal as your characters!

CHECK-IN

Think about your progress over the last four weeks. On the line below, list several adjectives that describe your feelings. Then rate the last four weeks on a scale of one to five (five being great).

1 2   3   4   5

....

1. Over the last four weeks, what have you most enjoyed about working toward your goals? What can you celebrate or feel good about?

....

....

....

2. What has been the most difficult for you? Is there anything you tried that didn't work? Did anything disappoint or surprise you?

....

....

....

3. How do you feel about your partner today? Is there anything you'd like to do differently in your relationship or in reaching your goals over the next four weeks?

....

....

....

Think about your progress over the last four weeks. On the line below, list several adjectives that describe your feelings. Then rate the last four weeks on a scale of one to five (five being great).

1 2 3 4 5

1. Over the last four weeks, what have you most enjoyed about working toward your goals? What can you celebrate or feel good about?

2. What has been the most difficult for you? Is there anything you tried that didn't work? Did anything disappoint or surprise you?

3. How do you feel about your partner today? Is there anything you'd like to do differently in your relationship or in reaching your goals over the next four weeks?

WEEK 21   Date ....

To work toward my goal, this week I will . . .

1 ....

....

....

2 ....

....

....

To help me be successful, I will need the following for myself and/or from my partner . . .

1 ....

....

....

2 ....

....

....

Write your partner a love letter telling them about the moment you *knew*. You can define that however you choose (e.g., the moment you knew you wanted to ask them on a date, kiss them, or ask them to move in with you). Try to include as many specific details as possible.

1

2

You find a winning lottery ticket for $1 million lying on the street one day. Will you . . .

a) Keep it and collect the money?
b) Try to find who lost it and return it to them?
c) Donate it to a charity organization?
d) Other

1   **2**

WEEK 22

Date ....

To work toward my goal, this week I will . . .

1 ....

....

....

2 ....

....

....

To help me be successful, I will need the following for myself and/or from my partner . . .

1 ....

....

....

2 ....

....

....

Answer the following multiple-choice questions.

What kind of date nights do you like?

a) Stay at home and cuddle
b) Eat at a fancy restaurant
c) Something spontaneous

① .... ② ....

Which is most important to you?

a) Sense of humor
b) Money
c) Cooking skills

① .... ② ....

Which destination would you love to take your partner on a trip to?

a) Italy
b) Walt Disney World
c) Alaska

① .... ② ....

What's one quality of yours that you think made your partner fall in love with you?

① ....
....

....

② ....
....

....

Date

To work toward my goal, this week I will . . .

1

2

To help me be successful, I will need the following for myself and/or from my partner . . .

1

2

What makes you feel most loved?

a) When someone surprises me with a gift
b) When someone compliments me or shows appreciation
c) When someone really listens to me
d) When someone gives me a hug or holds my hand
e) When someone does a chore for me that I hate doing

Imagine you're going on an exciting trip, but your flight is delayed a few hours. Do you shrug, panic, or demand to be put on another flight?

SAVE THE DATE (Night)

Get pampered! Have a spa night at home by giving each other massages or taking a bubble bath. Or you can schedule a whole day at a local spa complete with a couple's massage and pedicures.

Date

To work toward my goal, this week I will . . .

1

2

To help me be successful, I will need the following for myself and/or from my partner . . .

1

2

Describe your childhood crush. Does your partner look like them? Do they have anything in common? If you can find a picture of them, show your partner and see what they think!

1

2

Do you and your partner have pet names for each other (e.g., honey, sweetheart, baby, or bunny)? Write them down and describe how they came to be. If not, brainstorm a few ideas below.

1

2

Think about your progress over the last four weeks. On the line below, list several adjectives that describe your feelings. Then rate the last four weeks on a scale of one to five (five being great).

1 2 3 4 5

1. Over the last four weeks, what have you most enjoyed about working toward your goals? What can you celebrate or feel good about?

2. What has been the most difficult for you? Is there anything you tried that didn't work? Did anything disappoint or surprise you?

3. How do you feel about your partner today? Is there anything you'd like to do differently in your relationship or in reaching your goals over the next four weeks?

CHECK-IN

Think about your progress over the last four weeks. On the line below, list several adjectives that describe your feelings. Then rate the last four weeks on a scale of one to five (five being great).

1 2 3 4 5

1. Over the last four weeks, what have you most enjoyed about working toward your goals? What can you celebrate or feel good about?

2. What has been the most difficult for you? Is there anything you tried that didn't work? Did anything disappoint or surprise you?

3. How do you feel about your partner today? Is there anything you'd like to do differently in your relationship or in reaching your goals over the next four weeks?

To work toward my goal, this week I will . . .

1

2

To help me be successful, I will need the following for myself and/or from my partner . . .

1

2

Some unexpected money comes your way. What do you do with it?

a) Spend it on something fun or a luxury trip
b) Buy gifts for loved ones
c) Pay off some debt
d) Save it for a rainy day

 ....

How does your partner inspire you? It could be their work ethic, their passion for helping others, their dedication to making you feel like a priority, or a trait they have that you envy.

To work toward my goal, this week I will . . .

....

....

....

....

....

....

To help me be successful, I will need the following for myself and/or from my partner . . .

....

....

....

....

....

....

What celebrity couple are you and your partner most like?

- **Beyoncé and Jay-Z**
- **John Krasinski and Emily Blunt**
- **Neil Patrick Harris and David Burtka**
- **Chrissy Teigen and John Legend**
- **Victoria and David Beckham**
- **Prince Harry and Meghan Markle**
- **Ellen DeGeneres and Portia de Rossi**

What is your favorite way to show affection for your partner in public? Holding hands? Kissing? Or do you prefer to keep a respectful (but still-loving) distance?

1 ....
....
....
....
....

2 ....
....
....
....
....

To work toward my goal, this week I will . . .

1

2

To help me be successful, I will need the following for myself and/or from my partner . . .

1

2

What do you hope other people would say about your relationship with your partner? Maybe it's something like "I can't imagine a happier couple" or "They're such a great team!" What do you hope others would take away from spending time with the two of you?

Imagine that your partner sends you a text saying they're having a bad day. What do you pick up at the store to make them feel better?

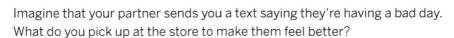

SAVE THE DATE *(Night)*

Put on your workout clothes and go sweat! You can take a yoga class, conquer a rigorous hike, or simply soak up the sun with a stroll around the park. Whatever it is, spend time getting active and *doing* something with each other.

Date ....

To work toward my goal, this week I will . . .

1 ....

....

....

2 ....

....

....

To help me be successful, I will need the following for myself and/or from my partner . . .

1 ....

....

....

2 ....

....

....

Is there a nighttime ritual that you and your partner could start tonight? This could be going to bed at the same time or texting each other the highlights and lowlights of your day.

1. ....
....
....

2. ....
....
....

What are three things your partner could not live without? Maybe it's their morning coffee, their phone, strawberry Pop-Tarts, or something else entirely. You might be on the list, too!

1. ....
....
....

2. ....
....
....

CHECK-IN

Think about your progress over the last four weeks. On the line below, list several adjectives that describe your feelings. Then rate the last four weeks on a scale of one to five (five being great).

1 2 3 4 5

1. Over the last four weeks, what have you most enjoyed about working toward your goals? What can you celebrate or feel good about?

2. What has been the most difficult for you? Is there anything you tried that didn't work? Did anything disappoint or surprise you?

3. How do you feel about your partner today? Is there anything you'd like to do differently in your relationship or in reaching your goals over the next four weeks?

CHECK-IN

Think about your progress over the last four weeks. On the line below, list several adjectives that describe your feelings. Then rate the last four weeks on a scale of one to five (five being great).

1 2 3 4 5

....

1. Over the last four weeks, what have you most enjoyed about working toward your goals? What can you celebrate or feel good about?

....

....

....

2. What has been the most difficult for you? Is there anything you tried that didn't work? Did anything disappoint or surprise you?

....

....

....

3. How do you feel about your partner today? Is there anything you'd like to do differently in your relationship or in reaching your goals over the next four weeks?

....

....

....

Date ....

To work toward my goal, this week I will . . .

1 ....
....
....
....

2 ....
....
....

To help me be successful, I will need the following for myself and/or from my partner . . .

1 ....
....
....
....

2 ....
....
....

Ask your partner to fill in the following blanks without reading the sentence below. Then insert each word into the sentence to see what you came up with.

1

Verb: ....

Verb: ....

Adjective: ....

Noun: ....

2

Verb: ....

Verb: ....

Adjective: ....

Noun: ....

"I (verb) and (verb) you. Whenever I lie next to you or hold you in my arms, I feel (adjective). My favorite place to be is wrapped up in a (noun)."

Imagine your partner has gone missing and you can't locate a photograph to give the police. How would you describe them? Think: height, weight, hair color, body type, and other unique physical characteristics.

1

....

....

....

2

....

....

....

Date ....

To work toward my goal, this week I will . . .

1 ....

....

....

2 ....

....

....

To help me be successful, I will need the following for myself and/or from my partner . . .

1 ....

....

....

2 ....

....

....

Try this intuition test with your partner. Maybe you can read each other's minds. (It's totally okay if you can't!) Think of three numbers between one and ten, and then see if your partner can guess each one!

Think about the best gift your partner has ever given you. Why was this particular gift so special? What did it make you feel or think?

1 ....
....
....

2 ....
....
....

SAVE THE DATE (Night)

Have a "five senses" date. Plan ways that you can use all five of your senses, like tasting something sour, smelling a candle or flower, or listening to music. Make it sweet or naughty.

Date ....

To work toward my goal, this week I will . . .

1 ....
....
....
....

2 ....
....
....

To help me be successful, I will need the following for myself and/or from my partner . . .

1 ....
....
....
....

2 ....
....
....

Rewrite Abraham Lincoln's famous Gettysburg Address to be about your relationship:

.... (months/years) ago, ... (name of Partner #1) and .... (name of Partner #2) brought forth, on this .... (place), a new .... (noun), conceived in .... (noun) and dedicated to the .... (noun) that we are .... (adjective or noun).

Imagine you and your partner won an all-expenses-paid trip around the world. Check the boxes below to indicate where you'd want to visit.

□ **Pyramids**

□ **Great Wall of China**

□ **Statue of Liberty**

□ **Eiffel Tower**

□ **Sydney Opera House**

□ **Leaning Tower of Pisa**

□ **Big Ben**

□ **Stonehenge**

□ **Mount Everest**

Date

To work toward my goal, this week I will . . .

1

2

To help me be successful, I will need the following for myself and/or from my partner . . .

1

2

You find yourself at a dance with your partner. Do you . . .

a) Drag them onto the dance floor until you're both exhausted?
b) Watch their personal items while they dance the night away?
c) Sit with them at a table and mock the other dancers?

If your partner were a fish, which kind would they be? Rainbow fish? Sword-fish? Whale? Draw what your partner would look like as a fish.

CHECK-IN

Think about your progress over the last four weeks. On the line below, list several adjectives that describe your feelings. Then rate the last four weeks on a scale of one to five (five being great).

1 2 3 4 5

1. Over the last four weeks, what have you most enjoyed about working toward your goals? What can you celebrate or feel good about?

2. What has been the most difficult for you? Is there anything you tried that didn't work? Did anything disappoint or surprise you?

3. How do you feel about your partner today? Is there anything you'd like to do differently in your relationship or in reaching your goals over the next four weeks?

CHECK-IN

Think about your progress over the last four weeks. On the line below, list several adjectives that describe your feelings. Then rate the last four weeks on a scale of one to five (five being great).

1 2 3 4 5

....

1. Over the last four weeks, what have you most enjoyed about working toward your goals? What can you celebrate or feel good about?

....

....

....

2. What has been the most difficult for you? Is there anything you tried that didn't work? Did anything disappoint or surprise you?

....

....

....

3. How do you feel about your partner today? Is there anything you'd like to do differently in your relationship or in reaching your goals over the next four weeks?

....

....

....

Date

To work toward my goal, this week I will . . .

1

2

To help me be successful, I will need the following for myself and/or from my partner . . .

1

2

Fill in the blanks with your partner's favorites. If you don't know, leave it blank and ask your partner!

Movie:

① .... ② ....

Dessert or snack:

① .... ② ....

Song, band, or musician:

① .... ② ....

Hobby:

① .... ② ....

Cousin or family member:

① .... ② ....

Beverage:

① .... ② ....

Relaxation activity:

① .... ② ....

Celebrity:

① .... ② ....

Answer the following questions about you and your partner:

Who's a better kisser?

1 .... **2** ....

Who's neater?

1 .... **2** ....

Who's funnier?

1 .... **2** ....

Who's the better driver?

1 .... **2** ....

Who's the better cook?

1 .... **2** ....

Who's better-looking?

1 .... **2** ....

Who's more honest?

1 .... **2** ....

Who's more adventurous?

① .... ② ....

Who's better at board games?

① .... ② ....

Who's a better listener?

① .... ② ....

SAVE THE DATE (Night)

Listen to some live music! Check out a concert, restaurant, bar, or salsa club. You can even livestream a band's show in your living room. If you're feeling particularly spunky, get up and dance together!

To work toward my goal, this week I will . . .

To help me be successful, I will need the following for myself and/or from my partner . . .

Many constellations are said to be heroes from Greek mythology, memorialized in the sky for their honorable acts. Write a myth about why you and your partner made it into the stars, then draw a picture of what your constellation would look like.

1 ....

....

....

....

....

2 ....

....

....

....

....

What animal best represents your partner's character traits? If you can't think of a creature that reminds you of them, write down ten adjectives that describe your partner.

1 ....

....

2 ....

....

To work toward my goal, this week I will . . .

To help me be successful, I will need the following for myself and/or from my partner . . .

Imagine you and your partner won the lottery. What would you buy first? Jot down some thoughts below, then see what your partner thinks.

1

2

Write down five compliments for your partner. These could be as small as "You always look so hot" or "Thank you for always making my tea." These could also be something like "Thank you for doing this journal with me" or "I love that you're my biggest fan."

1

2

Date ....

To work toward my goal, this week I will . . .

1 ....

....

....

....

2 ....

....

....

To help me be successful, I will need the following for myself and/or from my partner . . .

1 ....

....

....

2 ....

....

....

Set a timer for one minute. In that time, write down as many words as you can using the letters in the word *relationship*. No cheating! The partner who comes up with the most words gets to pick where you go for your next meal.

1

2

Imagine that you and your partner have been implicated in a crime you didn't commit and must go on the run. Where do you hide? How do you change your appearance? What are your new identities?

1

2

CHECK-IN

Think about your progress over the last four weeks. On the line below, list several adjectives that describe your feelings. Then rate the last four weeks on a scale of one to five (five being great).

1 2 3 4 5

....

1. Over the last four weeks, what have you most enjoyed about working toward your goals? What can you celebrate or feel good about?

....

....

....

2. What has been the most difficult for you? Is there anything you tried that didn't work? Did anything disappoint or surprise you?

....

....

....

3. How do you feel about your partner today? Is there anything you'd like to do differently in your relationship or in reaching your goals over the next four weeks?

....

....

....

CHECK-IN

Think about your progress over the last four weeks. On the line below, list several adjectives that describe your feelings. Then rate the last four weeks on a scale of one to five (five being great).

1 2 3 4 5

1. Over the last four weeks, what have you most enjoyed about working toward your goals? What can you celebrate or feel good about?

2. What has been the most difficult for you? Is there anything you tried that didn't work? Did anything disappoint or surprise you?

3. How do you feel about your partner today? Is there anything you'd like to do differently in your relationship or in reaching your goals over the next four weeks?

To work toward my goal, this week I will . . .

To help me be successful, I will need the following for myself and/or from my partner . . .

Create a list of trivia questions for your partner to guess. Here are some examples to inspire you: "Where did I go to high school?" "What did I want to be when I grew up?" "Where do I want to retire?"

1 ....

....

....

....

2 ....

....

....

....

If your partner were a vampire, would you want to let them turn you into one, so you could be vampires together for eternity? Or would you rather enjoy your life with them while you could and die of old age?

1 ....

....

....

....

2 ....

....

....

....

WEEK 38

To work toward my goal, this week I will . . .

1 ....

....

....

2 ....

....

....

To help me be successful, I will need the following for myself and/or from my partner . . .

1 ....

....

....

2 ....

....

....

See if you can answer the following tricky questions about your partner!

What is your partner's most prized possession?

1 _____ 2 _____

If your partner were home alone, what would they do?

1 _____ 2 _____

What is their most hated chore?

1 _____ 2 _____

What makes them furious?

1 _____ 2 _____

What always makes them laugh?

1 _____ 2 _____

Your partner calls you at 3:00 a.m. to pick them up. Why do they need a ride? Where are they most likely to be? Do you pick them up or send a taxi?

1 _____

_____

2 _____

_____

_____

WEEK 39

Date ....

To work toward my goal, this week I will . . .

....

....

....

....

2

....

....

....

To help me be successful, I will need the following for myself and/or from my partner . . .

....

....

....

....

....

....

....

Fill out the following *this or thats* about your partner. If there are any you aren't sure about, leave them blank and ask your partner.

Cats or dogs?

1 ....

2 ....

Sweet or salty?

1 ....

2 ....

Hot or cold?

1 ....

2 ....

Concert or theater?

1 ....

2 ....

City or country?

1 ....

2 ....

Life of the party or wallflower?

1 ....

2 ....

Action movie or romantic comedy?

1 ....

2 ....

Early riser or night owl?

1 ....

2 ....

Write down a compliment about something your partner did for you recently. Be specific.

1

2

SAVE THE DATE (Night)

Do a "crawl." Choose one food item—like beer, ice cream, or appetizers—that you could order at multiple places. Pop in and out of each place to taste each sample, or order in and try them all at home.

To work toward my goal, this week I will . . .

 ....

....

....

 ....

....

....

To help me be successful, I will need the following for myself and/or from my partner . . .

 ....

....

....

 ....

....

....

Write "over" or "under" next to the following statements, and then see if you're correct!

My partner has three pairs of shoes.

1 _____ 2 _____

My partner has received one speeding ticket.

1 _____ 2 _____

My partner got their first job when they were eighteen.

1 _____ 2 _____

My partner has had two cars in their lifetime.

1 _____ 2 _____

Write down a good-natured roast of your partner. For example: "Nick is almost perfect, but you should have seen all of the holes in his socks when we started dating."

1 _____
_____

2 _____
_____

CHECK-IN

Think about your progress over the last four weeks. On the line below, list several adjectives that describe your feelings. Then rate the last four weeks on a scale of one to five (five being great).

1 2 3 4 5

....

1. Over the last four weeks, what have you most enjoyed about working toward your goals? What can you celebrate or feel good about?

....

....

....

2. What has been the most difficult for you? Is there anything you tried that didn't work? Did anything disappoint or surprise you?

....

....

....

3. How do you feel about your partner today? Is there anything you'd like to do differently in your relationship or in reaching your goals over the next four weeks?

....

....

....

CHECK-IN

Think about your progress over the last four weeks. On the line below, list several adjectives that describe your feelings. Then rate the last four weeks on a scale of one to five (five being great).

1 2 3 4 5

1. Over the last four weeks, what have you most enjoyed about working toward your goals? What can you celebrate or feel good about?

2. What has been the most difficult for you? Is there anything you tried that didn't work? Did anything disappoint or surprise you?

3. How do you feel about your partner today? Is there anything you'd like to do differently in your relationship or in reaching your goals over the next four weeks?

WEEK 41

Date ....

To work toward my goal, this week I will . . .

1 ....

2 ....

To help me be successful, I will need the following for myself and/or from my partner . . .

1 ....

2 ....

Draw a picture below of your partner's silliest fear. It could be spiders crawling into their mouth while they're sleeping, a shark attack, or even cotton balls. Whatever it is, draw it!

What is something you would like to do but haven't done yet? Brainstorm how your partner could support you in doing it. Then write down something your partner would like to do but hasn't done yet. How would they like you to support them?

To work toward my goal, this week I will . . .

To help me be successful, I will need the following for myself and/or from my partner . . .

Would your partner rather be a singer, dancer, musician, movie star, news anchor, influencer, or reality TV star? Why? Do you think they'd love being famous, or not so much?

1

2

What is something you've always wondered about your partner but haven't gotten around to asking yet? If you'd like to ask them now, write it below. If you're not ready yet or can't think of something, write what you're excited to learn about them in the future.

1

2

To work toward my goal, this week I will . . .

1

2

To help me be successful, I will need the following for myself and/or from my partner . . .

1

2

When you have a bad day, what would make you feel better?

a) A long hug or cuddle on the couch
b) Your partner picking up your favorite dessert
c) Your partner telling you how much they love you
d) Your partner making you a meal
e) Venting to your partner

If you were reincarnated into someone or something else, what would it be?
For example, you could be a goat, a billionaire, or maybe a redwood tree.

SAVE THE DATE (Night)

Go stargazing! Find a park that is open at night or set up chairs in your backyard, then look up. You could even download a stargazing app and try it out from the comfort of your living room.

To work toward my goal, this week I will . . .

To help me be successful, I will need the following for myself and/or from my partner . . .

What is something you wish you and your partner did together more often?

1 ....

....

....

2 ....

....

....

Imagine a zombie outbreak occurs in your town. You and your partner must do everything you can to survive. What are each of your strengths and weaknesses? Who do you ally with and what weapons will you use to defend yourselves? How will you get food? And most important, who's more likely to survive: you or your partner?

1 ....

....

....

....

2 ....

....

....

....

CHECK-IN

Think about your progress over the last four weeks. On the line below, list several adjectives that describe your feelings. Then rate the last four weeks on a scale of one to five (five being great).

1 2 3 4 5

....

1. Over the last four weeks, what have you most enjoyed about working toward your goals? What can you celebrate or feel good about?

....

....

....

2. What has been the most difficult for you? Is there anything you tried that didn't work? Did anything disappoint or surprise you?

....

....

....

3. How do you feel about your partner today? Is there anything you'd like to do differently in your relationship or in reaching your goals over the next four weeks?

....

....

....

CHECK-IN

Think about your progress over the last four weeks. On the line below, list several adjectives that describe your feelings. Then rate the last four weeks on a scale of one to five (five being great).

1 2 3 4 5

1. Over the last four weeks, what have you most enjoyed about working toward your goals? What can you celebrate or feel good about?

2. What has been the most difficult for you? Is there anything you tried that didn't work? Did anything disappoint or surprise you?

3. How do you feel about your partner today? Is there anything you'd like to do differently in your relationship or in reaching your goals over the next four weeks?

Date ....

To work toward my goal, this week I will . . .

1 ....
....
....
....

2 ....
....
....
....

To help me be successful, I will need the following for myself and/or from my partner . . .

1 ....
....
....
....

2 ....
....
....
....

A "new soul" focuses on what's fun and unfamiliar, while an "old soul" takes a more wise and pragmatic approach to life. Are you an old or a young soul? What makes you think that? What about your partner?

1

2

If you could only wear one outfit every single day for an entire year, what would it be? Describe it in detail, down to the particulars of which shoes and socks. (Don't worry, it would be washed between uses.)

1

2

To work toward my goal, this week I will . . .

1

2

To help me be successful, I will need the following for myself and/or from my partner . . .

1

2

Remember the *Wizard of Oz*? Describe whether your partner is more of a Scarecrow (wants a brain), Tin Man (wants a heart), or Cowardly Lion (wants courage). Which character are you, and why? Do you wish you related more to a different character?

1

2

If you had three wishes and could only use them on your partner and your relationship, what would they be? You have 30 seconds to decide. (And no, you can't wish for more wishes!)

1

2

Date ....

To work toward my goal, this week I will . . .

....

....

....

....

....

....

To help me be successful, I will need the following for myself and/or from my partner . . .

....

....

....

....

....

....

What is something that you know is silly, but you believe in anyway? For example, maybe you believe in Bigfoot, mermaids, elves, dragons, or unicorns. What do you think it says about you that you still believe?

1

2

SAVE
THE DATE (Night)

Do a DIY project together. It always feels good to complete something, so pick something you can finish in one day. Think rehabbing furniture, making photo coasters, or upcycling something you already have around.

What is a place that you would like to take your partner to? Sketch a picture of the place below. Think about when you would like to take your partner, then write down a date that you plan to take them by.

1

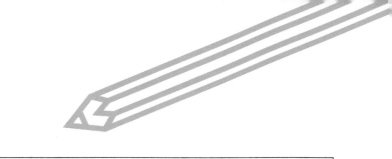

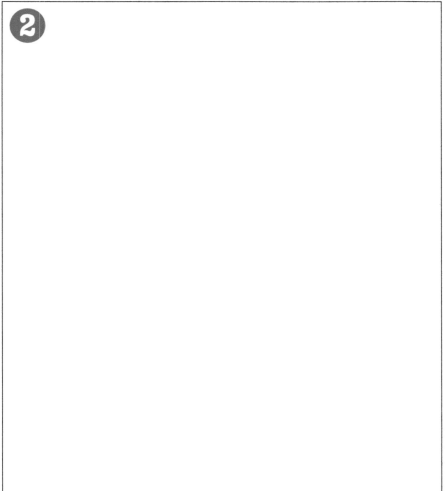

WEEK 48

Date ....

To work toward my goal, this week I will . . .

1 ....
....
....

2 ....
....
....

To help me be successful, I will need the following for myself and/or from my partner . . .

1 ....
....
....

2 ....
....
....

In the heart below, write down all the things your partner loves. Think about family members, friends, activities, passions, and—of course—you!

Write a short story in third person about how you and your partner met. For example: "Shelly and Eric sat across from each other on their very first date. Shelly was a petite brunette with stunning blue eyes, whereas Eric's biceps were nearly popping out of his black T-shirt . . ."

1

2

CHECK-IN

Think about your progress over the last four weeks. On the line below, list several adjectives that describe your feelings. Then rate the last four weeks on a scale of one to five (five being great).

1 2 3 4 5

1. Over the last four weeks, what have you most enjoyed about working toward your goals? What can you celebrate or feel good about?

2. What has been the most difficult for you? Is there anything you tried that didn't work? Did anything disappoint or surprise you?

3. How do you feel about your partner today? Is there anything you'd like to do differently in your relationship or in reaching your goals over the next four weeks?

CHECK-IN

Think about your progress over the last four weeks. On the line below, list several adjectives that describe your feelings. Then rate the last four weeks on a scale of one to five (five being great).

1 2 3 4 5

....

1. Over the last four weeks, what have you most enjoyed about working toward your goals? What can you celebrate or feel good about?

....

....

....

2. What has been the most difficult for you? Is there anything you tried that didn't work? Did anything disappoint or surprise you?

....

....

....

3. How do you feel about your partner today? Is there anything you'd like to do differently in your relationship or in reaching your goals over the next four weeks?

....

....

....

To work toward my goal, this week I will . . .

To help me be successful, I will need the following for myself and/or from my partner . . .

Your love story is so amazing that the bigwigs in Hollywood are making a movie about it! Who would play you and your partner? Imagine which actors would play the other people in your life that have had a role in your relationship.

1 ....

....

....

2 ....

....

....

Play tic-tac-toe together, but instead of using Xs and Os, use the first letter of each of your names. Whoever wins two out of three games gets to pick the next movie or show you watch together.

Date ....

To work toward my goal, this week I will . . .

1 ....
....
....

2 ....
....
....

To help me be successful, I will need the following for myself and/or from my partner . . .

1 ....
....
....

2 ....
....
....

Would you rather . . .

Ride in a hot-air balloon or scuba dive?

① .... ② ....

Be three years older or five years younger?

① .... ② ....

Live without TV or a phone?

① .... ② ....

Be smart or kind?

① .... ② ....

Have a job you love with low pay, or a job you hate with an amazing salary?

① .... ② ....

Never have you ever:

Ridden a horse ① .... ② ....

Played a tuba ① .... ② ....

Owned a house ① .... ② ....

Eaten French fries with mayonnaise ① .... ② ....

Jumped on a trampoline ① .... ② ....

WEEK 51

Date ....

To work toward my goal, this week I will . . .

1 ....

....

....

2 ....

....

....

To help me be successful, I will need the following for myself and/or from my partner . . .

1 ....

....

....

2 ....

....

....

How old were you when you stopped believing in the Tooth Fairy, Santa Claus, or the Easter Bunny? If your family didn't subscribe to these beliefs, were there other childhood stories you later found out were not true? Write down how you found out the truth, or how you think it might have happened. Compare your answers.

1

2

Imagine an asteroid is set to hit Earth. You and your partner have exactly one day left to live. What do you do? Where do you go? How will you make the most of it?

1

2

To work toward my goal, this week I will . . .

1

2

To help me be successful, I will need the following for myself and/or from my partner . . .

1

 2

What is your partner's best personality trait? Why? How does it complement a personality trait of yours?

1

2

SAVE THE DATE (Night)

Book a room at a quaint bed-and-breakfast or swanky downtown hotel. You can also create your own staycation by staying home and sharing a special meal. Write down a list of 52 things you love about your partner, then share it with them.

Write a song dedicated to your partner. If you'd like some extra inspiration, you can listen to "In Spite of Ourselves" by John Prine and Iris DeMent and set your own lyrics to that tune.

②

REFLECTIONS & FINAL THOUGHTS

Congratulations! You and your partner have done something amazing for your relationship by completing this journal together. Select one of you to be the "scribe," and answer the following questions together. These will help you both reflect on your progress and think about the future.

1. What did you accomplish that you're most proud of?

_____

_____

_____

_____

_____

_____

2. How did your relationship change as a result of working through this journal together?

_____

_____

_____

_____

_____

_____

3. What did you find difficult or surprising about working together to complete your goals?

_____

_____

_____

_____

_____

_____

_____

4. How have things changed between you since you started this journal? Did this process help make you more of a team?

_____

_____

_____

_____

_____

_____

_____

5. What do you wish you'd done differently when you started this journal? Why?

_____

_____

_____

_____

_____

_____

_____

_____

6. Did you and your partner complete all of your goals? If not, what were your obstacles? What is your plan to complete your goals in the future?

_____

_____

_____

_____

_____

_____

_____

_____

7. Do you have future goals to work on together? If so, what are they and how do you plan to work toward them together?

_____

_____

_____

_____

_____

_____

_____

_____

_____

_____

_____

_____

By supporting each other in completing your shared relationship goals, you've taken a valuable step toward ensuring that you have a healthier and happier relationship. Keep working on goals together and you will continue to strengthen your relationship.

Good luck!

Resources

***Atomic Habits* by James Clear:** This book is a definitive guide on how to break bad habits and adopt new ones in a way that's manageable and easy.

***Attached* by Dr. Amir Levine and Rachel S. F. Heller:** Learning your attachment style can be integral in understanding how you approach relationships. This book helps people move toward secure attachment.

***Better Than Before* by Gretchen Rubin:** Rubin breaks down current research on developing habits (good and bad) and gives simple tools to help you achieve your goals.

***Couple Skills* by Matthew McKay, Patrick Fanning, and Kim Paleg:** This book provides actionable exercises to master every skill a couple should have. This is a great book for continuing to set goals.

***Grateful in Love* by Tara Blair Ball:** Gratitude is an amazing practice. This guided journal helps you adopt the life-changing practice of gratitude and apply it to your relationship.

Habitify: Habit-tracking is a way to make yourself accountable for developing new habits and reaching your goals. This app allows you to track habits on your phone.

***Hold Me Tight* by Dr. Sue Johnson:** Based on emotionally focused therapy, this book helps you and your partner connect more deeply, move through disagreements, and heal unhealthy patterns.

Love Nudge: This app helps you and your partner learn your individual love languages. Use the app to set small, reasonable goals and fill each other's "love tank" every day.

References

Boogaard, Kat. "How to Write SMART Goals." Work Life by Atlassian. December 26, 2021. atlassian.com/blog/productivity/how-to-write-smart-goals.

Corporate Finance Institute. "SMART Goals." Accessed March 20, 2022. corporatefinanceinstitute.com/resources/knowledge/other/smart-goal.

Mind Tools. "SMART Goals: How to Make Your Goals Achievable." March 9, 2016. mindtools.com/pages/article/smart-goals.htm.

Tartakovsky, Margarita. "A Simple Tool for a More Meaningful Relationship." Psych Central. May 14, 2015. psychcentral.com/blog/a-simple-tool-for-a-more-meaningful-relationship#1.

University of California Office of the President. "SMART Goals: A How to Guide." 2016. ucop.edu/local-human-resources/_files/performance-appraisal/How%20to%20write%20SMART%20Goals%20v2.pdf.

ACKNOWLEDGMENTS

Many thanks to the team at Callisto Media, who are always a delight to work with, as well as all the clients I've worked with throughout the years. Last but never least, thank you to my wonderful husband, Brian, my biggest fan and my greatest love.

ABOUT THE AUTHOR

Tara Blair Ball is a certified relationship coach and author of *Grateful in Love: A Daily Gratitude Journal for Couples*. Ball specializes in helping individuals and couples go from toxic to happy. She has a bachelor's degree (Rhodes College, 2008) and a master's degree (University of Memphis, 2012), along with coaching cer-tifications (Transformation Academy, CTAA). She lives outside Memphis, Tennessee, with her husband, Brian, and their four children. If you want to discover other tools for healing and improving the relationships in your life, find her on Instagram and TikTok @tara.relationshipcoach or her website, tararelationshipcoach.com.